D1738825

PORTS

MOTOCROSS RACING

By K. A. Hale

🌐 WORLD BOOK

BIGFOOT BOOKS

The Quest for Discovery Never Ends

This edition is co-published by agreement between
Kaleidoscope and World Book, Inc.

Kaleidoscope Publishing, Inc.
6012 Blue Circle Drive
Minnetonka, MN 55343 U.S.A.

World Book, Inc.
180 North LaSalle St., Suite 900
Chicago IL 60601 U.S.A.

Kaleidoscope ISBNs
978-1-64519-066-0 (library bound)
978-1-64494-147-8 (paperback)
978-1-64519-167-4 (ebook)

World Book ISBN
978-0-7166-4359-3 (library bound)

Library of Congress Control Number
2019938878

Printed in the United States of America.

**FIND ME
IF YOU CAN!**

Bigfoot lurks within
one of the images in
this book. It's up to
you to find him!

TABLE OF
CONTENTS

CHAPTER 1

FUN FACT
It takes 500 truckloads of dirt to build a motocross track from scratch!

RACING TO VICTORY

Hamoody has spent all day at the track. But his day isn't over. Hamoody is a motocross racer. Motocross racers compete on dirt bikes, which are a type of motorcycle. They speed around dirt tracks and jump over obstacles.

Hamoody got here early this morning. He walked the track. He studied the jumps and turns. Then he practiced.

Riders should stay in their line. Otherwise, they could crash with other people.

He worked on staying in his line. It's not good to zigzag. He tested the jumps on the course.

Soon it was time for his first moto, or race. Racers ride in two motos. Each moto is fifteen minutes. Judges combine the scores from the two motos. His first moto was okay. He got fourth place. Now his second one is about to begin. He wants to do better this time.

Hamoody lines up at the starting gate. Ten other racers line up with him. Both of his feet are on the ground. They're in front of the foot pegs. He revs his bike. He bounces to warm up the tires. His right hand is on the front brake. His left hand is on the **clutch**. As soon as he lets go of the brake, the bike will go.

The gate falls back toward Hamoody. He takes off! Some people try to jump the gate too early. Their wheels get stuck in the metal bars. Hamoody knows better. He gets a good start. He has a lead on most of the other racers.

There are ruts in the dirt. They make it harder to ride. There are lots of jumps and turns. The track starts with a **berm turn**. Hamoody puts his leg out to help him steer. Then there are whoops. He goes through these small hills on his back wheel. Hamoody flies through his jumps. He completes **step-ups** and **step-downs**. He soars over **doubles**. He misses a jump. But he can try on the next lap.

Tricks like sticking a leg out around a turn can help a motocross racer succeed in a race.

The flagger waves a yellow flag. That means there's a problem on the track. Riders can't pass or jump. They have to ride carefully. Hamoody slows down. He hopes no one is hurt. Motocross is a dangerous sport. Riders run into each other. They fall off their bikes. They can crash out of a jump.

Finally, Hamoody nears the finish line. He wins the race! His parents are at the finish line. He comes second overall for the day. That's awesome! Hamoody loves motocross racing. He hopes to go pro someday.

Motocross racers have to be careful. They can be injured if they fall or crash.

CHAPTER 2

FROM SCRAMBLES TO STADIUMS

George starts his motorcycle. The year is 1947. He is from Great Britain. But today George is in the Netherlands. He's about to ride in the first international motocross championship.

Motocross racing started in Great Britain. Races were called scrambles. The first official scramble was in 1924.

Scrambles were run in natural landscapes. Then World War II (1939–1945) started. Competitions had to stop. But motorcycle companies kept making bikes. They built them for the military.

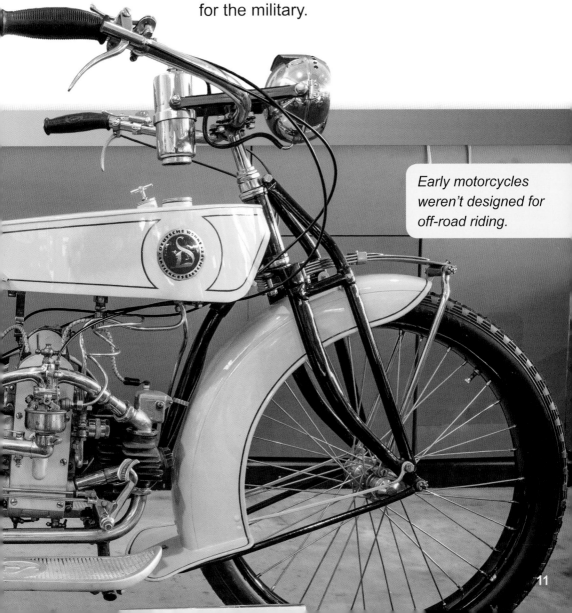

Early motorcycles weren't designed for off-road riding.

MOTOCROSS

RACING RECORDS

Most supercross wins of all time

Jeremy McGrath, 72 wins

First rider with a perfect season

Ricky Carmichael, 2002 and 2004

Most AMA wins of all time (motocross and supercross)

Ricky Carmichael, 150 wins

Youngest rider to win a supercross competition

Marty Tripes, 16 years old (1974)

First X Games Moto X Racing gold medalist

Ricky Carmichael, 2007

When the war ended, even more people raced motorcycles. They were affordable. The sport spread across Europe. Countries that had fought each other in the war had something in common. Soon, the sport was called motocross. *Motocross* comes from the French word for motorcycle, *motocyclette.* It's paired with *cross-country.*

The race begins. George takes off! The ride is bumpy. His bike doesn't absorb shock well. But motocross races are inspiring change. Motorcycles will improve over the years. They'll have **suspension** systems to help them drive better off-road. But George doesn't mind the bouncing. It's part of the fun.

The first motocross racers didn't have dirt bikes with suspension for off-road riding, but the riders kept racing and the bikes kept improving.

By 1960, Americans were familiar with the sport. But a man named Edison Dye changed everything. Dye worked for a motorcycle company. He wanted to show Americans the European style of motocross. Europe had large competitions. He thought Americans would like that. He thought it would make them buy more motorcycles.

Dye organized races. At first, European athletes came to the United States. Dye convinced them to come race. Eventually, Dye's plan worked. Americans wanted to ride like the European racers. They bought Dye's motorcycles. Over time, Americans became strong competitors. In 1972, the first stadium motocross race was held. Athletes raced at the Los Angeles Coliseum in California. This type of race turned into supercross.

Today, motocross is popular for people of all ages and skill levels. There are many competitions for pros. Motocross came to the X Games in 2007. Supercross has its own events. Monster Energy **AMA** Supercross is one of the biggest. There are also **amateur** races. One is the AMA Amateur National Motocross Championship. It's also called Loretta Lynn's.

FUN FACT

Loretta Lynn's is held on singer Loretta Lynn's ranch in Tennessee.

A perfect season happens when a rider wins each moto.

MOTOCROSS VS. SUPERCROSS

Motocross and supercross are the most popular dirt bike racing styles. They are similar. But there are still some big differences. Supercross is done inside arenas. The tracks are smaller. They're also man-made. Motocross is done outside. The tracks are built on natural land. Riders can compete in both.

CHAPTER 3

Protective motocross gear comes in many different colors and styles.

BIKES AND GEAR

The alarm goes off. Olivia jumps out of bed. It's race day! She runs to her closet. Motocross racers need special gear. She puts on her body armor. It's made of special foam. It's light and easy to move in. The armor protects her back and chest. It also pads her arms. Next comes her jersey. It has long sleeves. It matches her pants. They are green and purple. Finally, she puts on her shoes. She wears steel-toed boots. They protect her feet.

Olivia finds her mom in the garage. Together, they load the bike into the truck. Olivia loves her bike. It's a KTM 65 SX. The bike is orange. Its frame is lightweight. And it has a powerful engine. That means she can go fast. The bike also has a **hydraulic** clutch. It makes it easier to switch gears.

KTM is known for the flashy orange color of its dirt bikes.

FUN FACT
The KTM 65 SX's top speed is about 50 miles per hour (80 km/h)!

READY
TO RACE

Full-face helmet

Goggles

Protective armor
(some types are
worn under a jersey)

Gloves

Clutch lever

Front fender

Fork

Engine

Steel-toed boots

Full-face helmets and goggles are essential motocross safety gear.

Olivia grabs her full-face helmet. It protects her head and mouth. It's the most important piece of safety gear. She also wears goggles. The goggles protect her eyes from **roost**.

"All right! We're loaded up," Olivia's mom says. "Are you ready?"

Olivia nods. She can't wait to race.

CHAPTER 4

BIG NAMES ON THE TRACK

It takes a lot to be called the greatest of all time. But there's a reason Ricky Carmichael has this nickname. He has won a lot of races. He's set dozens of records. Carmichael has more motocross wins than any other racer. He's won 102 national titles. He entered the AMA Motorcycle Hall of Fame in 2013. Now, Carmichael is retired. He helps teach young riders how to race.

Ricky Carmichael had an extraordinary motocross racing career.

In 2015, Vicki Golden became the first woman to qualify for a supercross final.

Vicki Golden started racing as a kid. When she was twelve, she was supposed to go to Loretta Lynn's with her dad. But her dad crashed. He was hurt badly. Vicki's mom wanted her to stop racing. But Vicki wasn't scared. She won Loretta Lynn's that year. She's been a leader ever since. She won three X Games gold medals. She was the first woman to compete at Moto X Best Whip. She won a bronze medal there. Golden shows that men aren't the only ones who can race motocross.

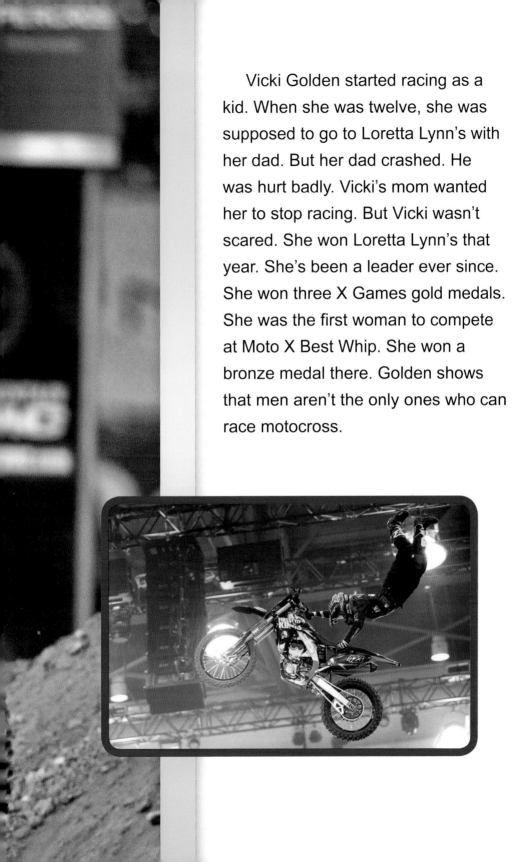

James Stewart Jr. got an early start in riding. His father took him on a dirt bike when he was only two days old. He started racing when he was four. People started calling him Bubba. The nickname stuck. Bubba won eleven AMA Amateur National Titles. He went pro in 2002. He was named Rookie of the Year. He and Carmichael are the only riders who have completed a perfect motocross season. The two are also tied for second-most supercross wins. Stewart was the first African American to dominate in motocross.

Motocross has come a long way since the first scramble in 1924. Today, racers around the world can compete. The bikes and the tracks have changed over time. But the excitement of motocross racing isn't going anywhere.

FUN FACT

Stewart had a reality TV show called *Bubba's World* from 2010 to 2011.

James "Bubba" Stewart is known for his signature Bubba Scrub move.

STARS OF
MOTOCROSS
RACING

RICKY CARMICHAEL

Ricky Carmichael is called the GOAT. This stands for greatest of all time. He won a total of 150 championships. He had two perfect motocross seasons. He also has the record for most riders lapped in a single moto. He lapped every single rider in a 2006 race. That was a total of thirty-nine racers.

VICKI GOLDEN

Vicki Golden is a trailblazer. She won four X Games medals. She was the first woman to qualify for a supercross final. In 2016, she transitioned from motocross racing to freestyle motocross. She performs tricks on her dirt bike.

JAMES STEWART JR.

James Stewart Jr. earned the nickname "Fastest Man on the Planet" for his motocross skills. He debuted his signature move, the Bubba Scrub, in 2002. He goes over a jump while turning the bike horizontally.

BEYOND
THE BOOK

After reading the book, it's time to think about what you learned.
Try the following exercises to jumpstart your ideas.

THINK

THAT'S NEWS TO ME. Vicki Golden won the Loretta Lynn's competition when she was twelve. How might news sources be able to fill in more detail about this? What new information could you find in news articles? Where could you go to find those sources?

CREATE

PRIMARY SOURCES. A primary source is a firsthand account of an event. Some examples of primary sources might be photographs, videos, or interviews. Make a list of different primary sources you might be able to find about motocross racing. What new information might you learn from these sources?

SHARE

SUM IT UP. Write one paragraph summarizing the important points from this book. Make sure it's in your own words. Don't just copy what is in the text. Share the paragraph with a classmate. Does your classmate have any comments about the summary or additional questions about motocross racing?

GROW

REAL-LIFE RESEARCH. What places could you visit to learn more about motocross racing? What other things could you learn while you were there?

RESEARCH NINJA

Visit *www.ninjaresearcher.com/0660* to learn how
to take your research skills and book report writing to the next level!

RESEARCH ·······································

DIGITAL LITERACY TOOLS

SEARCH LIKE A PRO
Learn about how to use search engines to find useful websites.

FACT OR FAKE?
Discover how you can tell a trusted website from an untrustworthy resource.

TEXT DETECTIVE
Explore how to zero in on the information you need most.

SHOW YOUR WORK
Research responsibly—learn how to cite sources.

WRITE ·······································

GET TO THE POINT
Learn how to express your main ideas.

PLAN OF ATTACK
Learn prewriting exercises and create an outline.

DOWNLOADABLE REPORT FORMS

FURTHER RESOURCES

BOOKS

Abdo, Kenny. *Motocross.* Abdo Publishing, 2018.

Adamson, Thomas K. *Motocross Racing.* Bellwether Media, 2016.

David, Jack. *Supercross Racing.* Bellwether Media, 2009.

WEBSITES

Factsurfer.com gives you a safe, fun way to find more information.

1. Go to www.factsurfer.com.

2. Enter "Motocross Racing" into the search box and click 🔍.

3. Select your book cover to see a list of related websites.

GLOSSARY

AMA: The AMA is the American Motorcycle Association. The AMA makes rules to keep motocross competitions fair.

amateur: An amateur is a person who does something for fun, not money. Hamoody is an amateur motocross racer.

berm turn: A berm turn is a banked turn, where the rider goes up the wall to turn. A berm turn can give riders more traction.

clutch: The clutch lets a rider shift gears. The clutch is controlled by a lever on the left handlebar.

doubles: Doubles are jumps made of two hills together. Riders take doubles as one jump, taking off from one hill and landing on another.

hydraulic: A hydraulic device is operated by pressure from liquid moving inside it. Olivia's hydraulic clutch makes it easier to switch gears.

roost: Roost is the dirt and rocks kicked up by another rider's bike. Riders wear goggles to protect themselves from roost.

step-downs: Step-downs are made from two jumps of different heights where riders jump down from a higher jump. The riders performed the step-downs on the track.

step-ups: Step-ups are made from two jumps of different heights where riders jump up to a higher landing. The rider prepared for the race's step-ups.

suspension: A vehicle's suspension is the system that supports it and absorbs shock from bumps and other conditions. The suspension kept him from feeling the impact of the whoops.

INDEX

PHOTO CREDITS

ABOUT THE AUTHOR

K. A. Hale is a writer and editor from Minnesota. She enjoys reading, writing, and playing with her dog.